SE

JOKES

FOR
BAD BOYS

TIM BRADBURY

Strathearn Publishing

TRADE DISTRIBUTION foulsham
THE PUBLISHING HOUSE, BENNETTS CLOSE,
CIPPENHAM, SLOUGH, BERKSHIRE, SL1 5AP

Strathearn publishing

PO Box 44, Slough, Berkshire, SL1 4YN

ISBN 0-572-02698-6

Printed in Great Britain by Cox & Wyman Ltd, Reading, Berkshire

What is the cleverest thing to have come from a woman's mouth?

Einstein's dick

What's white and wriggles across a dance floor?

Come dancing

What animal has a cunt halfway up its back?

A police horse.

What do you call a lesbian with thick fingers?

Well hung.

Why was Barbie banned from the toy cupboard?

She kept sitting on Pinocchio's face and saying, 'Lie to me, you bastard.'

Why was the blonde sacked from the sperm bank?

She was drinking on the job.

What do you call a fanny on top of a fanny on top of a fanny on top of a fanny?

A block of flaps.

What do you call a Serbian prostitute?

Slobberdown Mecockyerbitch.

What do you call a Pakistani lesbian?

Minjita.

෴෴෴෴෴෴෴෴෴෴෴෴෴෴෴

How do you stop a dog from shagging your leg?

Pick him up and suck his cock.

A woman went into a pub
and asked for a double entendre.

So the barman gave her one.

Why don't gypsies use condoms?

*Because they've got
crystal balls and can see when
they're coming.*

What do you call a blonde with a ten pound note on her head?

All you can eat under a tenner.

What does a gynaecologist have in common with a pizza delivery man?

They both get to smell the goods but they're not allowed to eat it.

What is the most irritating part of a blonde's vagina?

The blonde.

Did you hear about the woman who fell asleep on the steps of a synagogue?

She woke up the following morning with a heavy Jew on her.

What did Donald Duck say to the prostitute?

Put it on my bill.

How do you find a fat girl's pussy?

*You flip through the folds of fat
until you smell shit,
then go back one.*

Why does a dog lick his arse?

Because he knows in five minutes he'll be licking your face.

What do you call a fat woman with a yeast infection?

A whopper with cheese.

What does a lonely
homosexual do
when he's horny?

*He shits in his hand
and jerks off.*

What do you get if you
cross a yeast infection with
an achy breaky heart?

An itchy twitchy crotch.

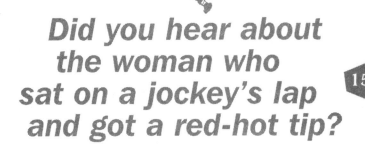

Did you hear about the woman who sat on a jockey's lap and got a red-hot tip?

How can you tell if two lesbians are twins?

They lick alike.

WHAT DOES A NECROPHILIAC HAVE IN COMMON WITH A FUR TRAPPER?

THEY BOTH HUNT FOR DEAD BEAVER.

What's red and white and sits in a tree all night?

A sanitary owl.

How is a pussy like a grapefruit?

The best ones squirt when you eat them.

What's the difference between spitting and swallowing?

About forty pounds of pressure on the back of the head.

What do you call a rabbit
with a bent dick?

Fucks Funny.

How do you know if you've got
a very high sperm count?

*Your girlfriend has to chew
before she can swallow.*

Q:
What do you call a Welshman
with a stick up his arse?

A:
Taffy apple.

**Did you hear about the
young man who was
thrown out of the Scouts
for eating Brownies?**

What is the definition of a
wicker box?

20

*It's what Elmer Fudd would
like to do to his favourite
movie star.*

What does a necrophiliac have in
common with a grave-digger?

THEY BOTH DIG DEAD PEOPLE'S HOLES.

Who is the world's greatest athlete?

**A man who finishes first and
third in a
masturbation contest.**

How can you tell if a woman
is really hot for you?

*When you put your hand
down her pants, it feels like
you're feeding a horse.*

What's another name
for a lesbian?

A vagetarian.

What do you call a
Welsh farmer with a couple
of sheep under his arms?

A pimp.

What's the difference between Gary Glitter and acne?

Acne doesn't come over your face until you're thirteen.

Did you hear about the man who got caught masturbating on a plane?

He was arrested for skyjacking.

Which of
Dickens' characters
liked to grab women's
tits?

David Cop-a-feel.

What's green,
has four legs and smells like
a woman's butt?

**The pool table in the White
House.**

Did you hear about
the man who became a
butcher because he
wanted to hear young girls
asking for a bit of tongue?

What is the smelliest
thing in the world?

A kipper's fanny.

What does a man
with a ten-inch dick
have for breakfast?

*Well, this morning
I had bacon, eggs and
orange juice.*

Did you hear about the Irish flasher?

He stepped forward from the police line-up

and said, 'That's the girl.'

HOW DO SHEPHERDS FIND SHEEP IN THE SNOW?

VERY REFRESHING.

Did you hear
about the 150lb man
who had 75lb testicles?

He was half nuts.

What do you call
a woman police officer with a
shaven pussy?

Cuntstubble.

Why are women's vaginas
so close to their arseholes?

*It's so that you can turn them over
and pick them up like a six-pack.*

What is the definition of a
perfect woman?

*She'd be three feet tall with
no teeth and a flat head to
rest your pint on.*

**How does a gay man fake
orgasm?**

*He grunts loudly,
pulls his cock out and spits on his
boyfriend's back.*

When is a pixie not a pixie?

30

When its head is up a fairy's skirt; then it's a goblin.

What do you do if a horny pit bull is shagging your leg?

Fake an orgasm.

*Bill and Ben, the flowerpot men,
were in bed one night...*

Bill said, 'Flobbalobbalobba.'

Ben said, 'If you really loved
me, you would have swallowed that.'

What is a dog's philosophy of life?

If you can't eat it or fuck it, piss on it.

HOW DO YOU MAKE A WOMAN SCREAM TWICE?

Fuck her up the arse and then wipe your cock on her curtains.

How do you know if a woman is macho?

She has to kick-start her vibrator.

Why can't you have driving
lessons and receive sex education
on the same day in Iraq?

It wears out the camel.

★ ★ ★ ★ ★ ★ ★

What's the definition
of trust?

*Two cannibals giving each
other a blow job*

.

What do a puppy and a near-sighted gynaecologist have in common?

THEY BOTH HAVE A WET NOSE.

How do Greeks separate
the men from the boys?

With a crowbar.

Why do hippos
fuck under water?

*Do you know how hard it is
to keep a 500-lb
pussy wet?*

What do Christmas trees and
priests have in common?

Their balls are just for decoration.

How can you tell if your girlfriend is frigid?

When you open her legs,
the lights go on.

What's the difference between a pussy and apple pie?

You can eat your mum's apple pie.

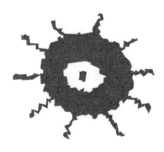

Why is having your cock sucked by an 80-year-old woman like walking on a tightrope?

You *really* don't want to look down.

What is the pharmaceutical name for Viagra?

MYCOXAFILLIN.

Why do tampons have string?
So you can floss after eating.

Why is a woman like take-away fried chicken?

*By the time you've finished with
the breast and thighs, all you're left with
is a greasy box to put your bone in.*

What is 69 + 69?

Dinner for four.

What is the definition of a bastard?

A man who screws his wife all night long with a three-inch dick, then kisses her goodbye the following morning with a ten-inch tongue.

What's green and eats nuts?

Herpes.

How do you know when a girl is too fat to fuck?

When you pull down her pants and her arse is still in them.

How do you recycle a
condom?

*Turn it inside out and
shake the fuck out of it.*

**What do you get if you cross
an onion with a donkey?**

**A piece of ass that'll bring
tears to your eyes.**

Did you hear about the leper who made the painful mistake of jerking off?

✖✖✖✖✖✖✖✖✖✖✖✖

How do you know if you're really ugly?

*Dogs shag your leg
with their eyes closed.*

✖✖✖✖✖✖✖✖✖✖✖✖

How do you recognise a tough woman?

She rolls her own tampons.

Why was the gay man
expelled from the leper colony?

Some bum split on him.

WHAT DID THE JEWISH CHILD MOLESTER SAY TO THE LITTLE BOY?

Do you wanna buy some candy?

What is the hardest thing to say when you have a cock in your mouth?

Don't come.

WHAT DO YOU GET IF YOU CROSS A PENIS WITH A POTATO?

A DICTATOR.

What's worse than silicon breasts?

A cardboard box.

Why is a pussy
like a warm toilet seat?

They both feel good,
but you can't help wondering who's
been there before you

What's the difference between
a blonde and a mosquito?

A mosquito will stop sucking
when you smack it.

What do you get
when
you cross an
elephant with a
dog?

A dead dog
with a twelve-inch
arsehole.

Did you hear about the girl
who had tits on her back?

*She was hideous to look at
but great fun to dance with.*

What do you call a man with a rabbit stuck up his arse?

Warren.

What's the difference between a drug pusher and a prostitute?

A prostitute can wash her crack and use it again.

What's the quickest way to clear a gents' toilet?

Say, 'Nice dick.'

WHAT'S GROSSER THAN GROSS?

A cheerleader suction-cupped to the floor.

Do you know why they call it the Wonderbra?

When you take it off, you wonder where her tits went.

How do you get rid of
unwanted pubic hair?

Cough... spit...

retch... spit...

**How can you tell if a young
Greek male is a gentleman?**

**He waits until the third date
before screwing his girlfriend's brother.**

Did you hear about the guy who was into sadism, necrophilia and bestiality?

He was flogging a dead horse.

What do instant cameras and condoms have in common?

They both capture the moment.

WHAT'S THE SIMILARITY BETWEEN A CARTON OF MILK AND A WOMAN?

**They both need
their flaps pulled back before
you get to the good bit.**

What's the definition of egghead?

It's what Mrs Dumpty gives to Humpty.

Have you heard about the new orgasm pill for women?

It comes with a sixteen-inch applicator.

How many animals
can you put into a
pair of knickers?

One ass, one beaver,
two calves,
a whole bunch of hares,
and a fish that nobody
can find.

How many cocksuckers does it take to change a light bulb?

Shut up and keep sucking.
You can change the fucking bulb once I've come.

58 Did you hear about the guy who bought his wife a new dress and a dildo?

He figured if she
didn't like the dress,
she could go fuck herself.

What is oral sex?

THE TASTE OF THINGS TO COME.

How do you know when you've had a good blow job?

When you have to burp her to get your balls back.

**Why are cowgirls
bow-legged?**
*A cowboy likes to eat
with his hat on.*

Have you heard about the new
ultra-sensitive condom?

It hangs around
after the man has left and
talks to the woman.

What's the difference between a genealogist and a gynaecologist?

One looks up your family tree and the other looks up your family bush.

What's the definition of eternity?

The time between when you come and when she leaves.

You have a donkey and
I have a rooster.
Your donkey eats my rooster's feet.
What do we have?

*Two feet of my cock
in your ass.*

What's the most dangerous part
of the San Francisco marathon?

Getting in the starting blocks.

Why do women have foreheads?

So you have somewhere to kiss them after you've come in their mouth.

Have you ever seen the serial number on a condom?

I guess you've never rolled it back that far.

We're not getting enough!

And we're certainly not getting it regularly!
C'mon guys – we need more jokes and one-liners.
If you don't perform there won't be another
collection!

If you hear a funny story and think that it would be good for our next collection, then just send it in.

If we publish your joke in the next book, we will acknowledge you as its author and send you a free copy containing your name in print.

You can then flash the book round the pub to show how famous you have become. And insist that those who wish to remain in your company buy you drinks in recognition of your achievement.

Yours for a laugh,

 ED. *Strathearn Publishing*

P.S. You'll find our address on the back of the title page. Where we have more than one submission of the same joke, then the first received will be given the credit.